Insights of the Spirit
Messages of Love

by

Jane Tucker

Copyright 2004 by Jane Tucker

Layout and Design by Tom and Jane Tucker

Second Edition: published 2016

Passages from this booklet may be copied and used for educational purposes; please contact the author directly for permission: janetucker@shaw.ca

Acknowledgement

Once again, my deepest gratitude to the late Sydney Banks, an ordinary working man who had a profoundly enlightening experience, uncovering the Three Universal Principles of Mind, Consciousness and Thought. Syd dedicated his life to sharing these Principles with anyone in need, helping untold numbers of people find hope, health and happiness within themselves. As he predicted, the mental health field is being transformed as these Principles are acknowledged, and this transformation is receiving international recognition and respect.

Syd's archived website, www.sydneybanks.org is a treasure that has been left virtually unchanged since his passing, and contains his last messages to the world. All of Syd's books, writings and recorded talks offer an incomparable opportunity to touch the infinite beauty, wisdom and love that lie within every human soul. The power of such an experience, and of these materials, cannot be overstated.

Whatever pleasure you may find in the thoughts expressed on these pages, please know that the inspiration was kindled by the inexpressible depth of what Syd found and shared, and his constant direction to "look within" for the answer.

Dedication

To my dear family, who inspire me
each and every day
and fill my heart with
endless gratitude.

To the beautiful souls at
the correctional facility in Maryland
where I had the privilege of
introducing the Principles via the
materials of Sydney Banks.
Much of this booklet
was inspired by their sharing.

Insights of the Spirit

Table Of Contents

Awakening...1
The Difference...2
Finding Freedom....................................3
Deeper Understanding........................4
Recognizing Truth.................................5
Change of Heart.....................................7
Truth Acknowledged............................9
Love is the Healer................................10
Change...11
Timing..12
Seeing Innocence................................13
Peace and Quiet..................................14
Treading Lightly...................................15
Our Inner Identity................................17
Neutrality..19
Oneness..20
Faith, Hope, Love.................................21
Going Home..22

Awakening

A breakthrough is a beautiful experience
for everyone who is touched by it.

When someone sees a new reality,
the old reality fades
like a dream in the light of day.

The whole world changes.

Instead of fear and anger,
peace and understanding fill the soul.

There is nothing more profound
or more positive.

A breakthrough inspires deepest gratitude
in the one experiencing it,
and in any fortunate enough
to knowingly witness such an event.

It is a gift for everyone.

The Difference

After a true breakthrough,
one rides the swells and dips of life's ocean
without fear of drowning.

Not even the strongest wind
can extinguish the candle of hope
burning quietly within one's heart.

No earthquake can shake
the rock-solid foundation of faith.

Though tears may come,
they do not bring despair.

New life begins.

~~Insights of the Spirit~~
Finding Freedom

We are not our past. Whatever has happened to us, whatever we have been through, it is now only a memory ~ a thought. That thought is only as real as the life we give to it, at this very moment.

There is Something Greater within us that heals all wounds. It is Love that heals, not time alone. People can carry hate throughout their whole lives until they turn within, and find the Love that overpowers it.

We have nothing to lose by letting go of the past, and everything to gain. Every single thing that has happened in our past can be a source of deeper understanding, once we see it from a higher level ~ once we are guided by Spirit rather than by our pain and fears.

We can find freedom from our past, and when we do, the way opens for sharing what we have found. The gratitude we feel inspires us to help others who are suffering ~ to show them there truly is a way out of the darkness.

The way is found within.

Deeper Understanding

"Everything happens for a reason."

When we go through pain and confusion
it does no good to wonder
about the "reasons why"
as we will never figure it out.

Only when we give up,
and accept what we are feeling
as evidence that we are human,
will we begin to understand.

Deeper understanding is always the answer,
and deeper understanding comes,
not from the intellect,
but from the Spirit.

Recognizing Truth

We all have the ability to recognize Truth when we hear it spoken. It isn't a matter of agreeing intellectually with what is said, it is deeper than that. It is that feeling inside, that knowing, that moment of connection with our inner wisdom. Then, we have no doubt. We are not merely believing what someone else says; we are acknowledging the Truth that we know.

But what if someone is telling us something that does not "ring true?" Although we might be tempted to argue, it makes more sense to remain calm, and listen more deeply.

If pressed to respond, a calmer state of mind will help us communicate without offending.

There are many personal truths, as everyone sees life from a particular point of view. We don't need to judge others if our truths do not agree.

As we learn to quiet down and listen to the knowledge that lies within, we deepen our spiritual connection to the Greater Truth that never changes -- the impersonal Truth that lies at the heart of all creation. This Inner Truth will comfort and guide us, in silence.

It is pointless to argue. The most effective way to help others is to live what we know. If we start to share and receive a negative reaction, it is probably time to be quiet.

What has been found cannot be lost. We all go off track sometimes, but what we have learned is always there, just waiting for us to quiet down enough to remember.

Change of Heart

If angry, sad or resentful thoughts rise up in our minds, clouding our happiness and peace of spirit, we can believe them and make them more real, or we can see them as illusion. The choice is ours, always.

If we feel we've been hurt, we may think we're protecting ourselves from further pain by "keeping our guard up." The mistake here is that we are relying on our ego (our delusional image of who we are) to protect us, instead of relying on our Inner Wisdom to guide us.

Everybody experiences pain in life. It happens when what we desire, or what we expect, is denied us. If it is a deep loss, it is natural that waves of grief will wash over us, at times, unexpectedly. If we let them come and let them go, without attaching negative thoughts to them, we will not be contaminated.

If we become angry and resentful and create a fixed image of "how things are" based on our pain, we create a world where that theme is central.

There are always two alternatives: living in Love or living in fear. Fearful thoughts can vanish in an instant, when the Truth within us unfolds. The Truth is Love so strong and so pure that nothing can harm it.

As Sydney Banks often said, we all get our "knocks" in life, no matter who we are. He called life a "contact sport" and it surely is. No one is immune from getting hurt, but we have a choice in how we respond.

Judgment and bitterness are not gifts of Truth, they are illusions that get in the way, postponing happiness. Faith in the ultimate goodness of life opens the door for happiness and healing.

~~Insights of the Spirit~~

Truth Acknowledged

There are times when pain is so strong we have no choice but to accept it, let it run its course, and know that it will pass, eventually.

What can lessen the intensity and help our good feelings to return, is Faith.

Faith is knowing that, ultimately, Life is Good.

Faith is remembering the Love that is inside us, the Love that has nurtured us, the Love that is beyond ego, personality, time and space.

Faith is remembering the blessings we have received, and the wisdom at our Core.

Everyone on earth experiences deep pain at one time or another. If we keep our sights set on the present moment, open our awareness to the beauty and joy we have Inside, in spite of the "cloud covering" we are experiencing, we are acknowledging Truth.

When Truth is acknowledged, it begins to transform our suffering into acceptance and understanding.

Love is the Healer

Love heals all wounds.
Find it deep in your soul.
Love is the answer.
In Love you are whole.

No matter what's happened
Or what you've been through
Love makes it vanish;
Love makes life new.

Listen, Dear One,
To the clear voice within
Your True Self is waiting
You're where Love begins.

Listen, Dear Friend,
And hear what is true
You are whole, you are worthy
And Love lives in you.

Change

Change can be scary. Even if what we're doing is painful and is obviously leading us deeper and deeper into trouble, we sometimes forget we have a choice, and so we stay where we are. We forget there could actually be a different way to live; we think the world of happiness and good fortune is meant for others, not us, and that we deserve to suffer.

Nothing could be farther from the truth. All we have to do is wake up to the fact that we are of Spiritual Essence, that there is nothing wrong with us at our core, that we have the strength and power within to overcome anything that has ever happened.

If you are ready to change, you will. There is nothing stronger than Truth, and when we align ourselves with what we know, inside, and trust that inner wisdom, it guides us toward health and happiness.

Timing

So much suffering comes from wanting things to happen on our time schedule, as opposed to allowing Life to unfold in its own perfect timing.

Impatience is closely related to greed --wanting to have what we want, now, and feeling upset or angry if we don't get it.

A simple, single change of thought can transform everything.

As we Realize Patience
As we Realize Gratitude
As we Realize Hope
We Know that our deepest
Heart's desires
Will be fully realized

When the time is right.

~~Insights of the Spirit~~

Seeing Innoncence

When someone acts unkindly, if we take it personally, we can be thrown into a downward spiral of anger, blame, and judgment. These negative thoughts can create greater conflict, misunderstanding, and unfortunate results.

The more aware we are, the less we are affected by others' actions. We may feel angry for a moment, but the anger fades as we realize we are losing touch with what has become so precious -- our peace of mind.

As wisdom returns, we may smile inwardly, seeing the innocence of the one who has "harmed" us -- realizing that we truly have not been harmed at all.

Instead of anger, we feel compassion for another soul who is, perhaps, blinded by thoughts of fear and confusion.

We are no longer at the mercy of outside circumstances.

Peace and Quiet

In our day to day lives, we often get swept up in currents of busy thinking. It can become such a habit to always be planning the future, or reviewing the past, that we don't even realize we're doing it.

Then, we are blessed with a reminder. It might be a long-awaited vacation -- a chance to get away from the pressures and obligations we create for ourselves -- and if we are very fortunate, we experience a calming of the mind.

Gazing up through tall trees to a starlit sky, we feel a peace descending. We realize that our constant stream of mental plans and details has been a distraction, and we allow our busy thinking to fall away. We feel freer and more relaxed.

An insight such as this doesn't have to come from a physical change of scene. It can happen anywhere, anytime we experience a moment of inner peace and quiet.

It can happen right now.

Treading Lightly

Everyone has low periods. We might be struck down by a cold, or some other illness. If we can feel grateful for the forced rest, we might at least find a reason to smile. It's amazing how a single thought can change our experience of reality -- even a reality of sickness.

For example, if my head aches, and my nose is stuffed up, and my throat is scratchy, and I haven't slept well, I have a choice. I can mentally bemoan my sorry condition, or I can see the humor in it. Which choice makes more sense? Which will make me feel better? The answer is obvious.

Every single experience that comes our way is an opportunity. What we make of that opportunity is up to us. The trick is not to take ourselves too seriously.

If we find ourselves becoming absorbed in negative thoughts, whether they be thoughts of self-pity, anger, fear, or whatever, we need to recognize that we are traveling down a slippery slope.

Unless we stop giving those thoughts energy, we will soon slide into a murky pool of misery. From such a place, it's impossible to see the world clearly.

Life is glorious! Even when we're sick, even when we're tired, even when we're in a situation that might seem, on the outside, to be very unfortunate. If we take the thoughts off ourselves, our worries, our woes, and allow our inner spirit to guide us up, our reality becomes transformed. We begin to see ourselves and others in innocence, and notice the love that is all around, just waiting for us to express it.

When we let go of our self-involved thoughts, we open up to beauty and sharing.

If I'm worried that I can't give enough to my children, all I can give them is my worries. If, instead, I am grateful to life, I will pass on to my children this feeling of gratitude. Even if I can't be with them now, I can share beautiful feelings with them on a spiritual level. As for the future, it's amazing how Life has a way of opening doors, when we are truly ready.

Our Inner Identity

No matter what point we are on in our journey, there is always more to find. This is what makes life fascinating. There is no end to discovering the mysteries of Mind, because Mind, like Life, is infinite. While we can all see ourselves as "only beginning" the journey, we can also realize that at some level, we are already there. Our destination lies within, and is always, as Sydney Banks often said, only "one thought away."

If we concentrate too much on how we are "not there yet," we deny the Truth of our inner identity. Yes, we have much yet to learn. Yes, we still fall into old habits at times. But inside, at our core, we are whole and perfect, and we have access to wisdom that will guide us without fail.

Once we have glimpsed this true, inner identity, life is never the same for us. No matter how many times we fall, we do not despair. We know that it is only our misguided thoughts that have led us astray; only tricks of the ego, trying to hide from us who we really are.

We are not our failings. We are not our fears. We are not our shortcomings. We are more than these things.

If we make a mistake, we can acknowledge it, make up for it if possible, and move on. We don't need to define ourselves by what we have done. We don't have to think that it will necessarily happen again. If we have learned something from the experience at a deep level, this will change how we act in the future.

If we find ourselves repeating a negative experience over and over, it is just life letting us know we need to go deeper, to quiet down our thinking and find more gratitude. This will lead us in the right direction, to a more aware conscious state where we will not find ourselves in that same predicament.

We have so much to be thankful for. There is no one who is not blessed.

Neutrality

Every moment of each day
is an opportunity.

If we hold on to attachments
about how life "ought to" unfold,
we set ourselves up
for disappointment.

When something beautiful happens,
that moment in itself
is reason to rejoice.

Oneness

At the deepest levels
of the Mystery
there are no words.

If we go to that place
of silence, within,
we find the Divine.

This Inner Communion
is denied to no one.

~~Insights of the Spirit~~

Faith

Faith is not limited to what we "think."

Faith is Knowing.

Hope

Hope is powerful.

Attachment to an outcome is not.

Attachment brings tension and worry.

Hope brings confidence and peace.

Love

Love is unconditional and everlasting.

Love depends on nothing; its Source is within.

Love travels faster than light,
and lights our way Home.

It is Here, Now, Forever.

~~Insights of the Spirit~~
Going Home

Nothing is more beautiful than seeing someone
who has been lost, become found.

It reawakens faith and hope and strengthens love.

It deepens our understanding like nothing else can.

It is humbling and joy-inspiring
and warming to the soul.

The more lost the person was,
the more the miracle is felt.

The more a heart opens, the more love fills it.

We have witnessed this for a reason.

It is a gift of the most meaningful kind;
we will never be the same.

The love we feel is its own reward.

One who has been through the fire
and survived is reborn.

Up from the ashes comes new life
and uncovered wisdom.

We rejoice and feel relief and know
that tomorrow is a new day.

We have the privilege to offer continued support
and Unconditional Love.

All here to share Love and nothing else.

~~Messages of Love~~

Mahalo

Printed in Great Britain
by Amazon